You shall call his name Jesus for he will save his people from their sins.

Matthew 1:21

You shall call his name _ _ _ _ _ _ for he will _ _ _ _

his people from their _ _ _ _ . _ _ _ _ _ _ _ 1:21

Seek first the kingdom of God and his righteousness.
Matthew 6:33

_ _ _ _ first the _ _ _ _ _ _ _ of _ _ _ and his
righteousness. _ _ _ _ _ _ _ 6:33

Come to me all who are weary and
I will give you rest. Matthew 11:28

_ _ _ _ to me all who are _ _ _ _ _ _ and I will
give you _ _ _ _. _ _ _ _ _ _ _ 11:28

All the multitude came to him and he taught them.
Mark 2:13

All the _ _ _ _ _ _ _ _ _ _ came to him and
he _ _ _ _ _ _ them. _ _ _ _ 2:13

Let the little children come to me and do not forbid them.
Mark 10:14

Let the _ _ _ _ _ _ children come to _ _
and do not forbid them. _ _ _ _ 10:14

Watch and pray, lest you enter into temptation.
Mark 14:38

_ _ _ _ _ _ and _ _ _ _, lest you enter into

_ _ _ _ _ _ _ _ _ _ _. _ _ _ _ 14:38

Jesus rebuked the wind and raging water and there was calm. Luke 8:24

Jesus rebuked the _ _ _ _ and _ _ _ _ _ _ water and there was _ _ _ _. _ _ _ _ 8:24

Consider the ravens. They neither sow nor reap and
God feeds them. Luke 12:24

Consider the _ _ _ _ _ _ . They neither _ _ _ nor
_ _ _ _ and God _ _ _ _ _ them. _ _ _ _ 12:24

God be merciful to me a sinner.

Luke 18:13

God be _ _ _ _ _ _ _ _ to me a _ _ _ _ _ _.

_ _ _ _ 18:13

For God so loved the world that he gave his only begotten Son, that whoever believes in him should not perish but have everlasting life. John 3:16

For God so _ _ _ _ _ the _ _ _ _ _ that he gave his only begotten Son, that whoever _ _ _ _ _ _ _ _ in him should not perish but have everlasting _ _ _ _. _ _ _ _ 3:16

I am the good shepherd. The good shepherd gives his life
for the sheep. John 10:11

I am the _ _ _ _ shepherd. The good _ _ _ _ _ _ _ _
gives his _ _ _ _ for the _ _ _ _ _. _ _ _ _ 10:11

I am the way, the truth and the life. No one comes to the Father, except through me. John 14:6

I am the _ _ _, the _ _ _ _ _ and the _ _ _ _.
No one comes to the Father, except through
me. _ _ _ _ 14:6

The man entered the temple with Peter and John – walking,
leaping and praising God. Acts 3:8

The _ _ _ entered the _ _ _ _ _ _ with Peter
and John – walking, _ _ _ _ _ _ _ and
_ _ _ _ _ _ _ _ God. _ _ _ _ 3:8

The Lord opened Lydia's heart to heed the things spoken by Paul.
Acts 16:14

The Lord _ _ _ _ _ _ _ Lydia's _ _ _ _ _ _ to heed the

things _ _ _ _ _ _ by _ _ _ _ . _ _ _ _ 16:14

Believe on the Lord Jesus Christ and you will be saved.
Acts 16:31

_ _ _ _ _ _ _ on the _ _ _ _ Jesus Christ and you
will be _ _ _ _ _ . _ _ _ _ 16:31

Jesus and the Bible

Go into all the world and preach the gospel to
every creature. Mark 16:15

_ _ into all the _ _ _ _ _ and _ _ _ _ _ _ the
_ _ _ _ _ _ to every _ _ _ _ _ _ _ _ .
_ _ _ _ 16:15

The Bible books I have done are:

Matthew ☐   Luke ☐   Acts ☐
Mark ☐   John ☐